T0130502

A Prayer Guide for Kids

KASEY JORDAN

To order additional copies of this book, contact:
Xlibris
1-888-795-4274
www.Xlibris.com
Orders@Xlibris.com

ISBN: Softcover   978-1-7960-4748-6
         EBook   978-1-7960-4747-9

Print information available on the last page

Rev. date: 07/22/2019

A Prayer Guide for Kids

Table of Contents

How to pray?

You have to pray over your food like this, "thank you God (our heavenly father) for our food I'm about to receive in Jesus (God's son) Amen.

Think of things, people and events that you are thankful for. Then you can start your prayer with words of thanks giving.

For starters. "Our father, who is in heaven, hallowed be your name, your kingdom come, your will be done, on earth as it is in heaven. Give us this day our daily bread and forgive us our trespasses, as we forgive those who trespass against us. And lead us not into temptation, but deliver us from evil, for God and his kingdom, his power, his glory, forever and ever."

Then after that you start to thank God for everything you have. Finally, you say Amen. (Something you say after every praying)

Times to pray

The best times to pray are when you just get home from school or when you have to pray over your food. You can also pray before you go to sleep and when you wake up. You can pray anytime!

No matter what's going on you can pray at anytime. Even if you're about to take a test. You can privately in your head pray asking God to help you pass. If you're walking or riding home, you can thank God for the good day you had. If you had a bad day, ask God to help you tomorrow.

What to pray about?

If you want something then just ask for it or if you don't need or want anything just thank God for all that he has already done for you. Don't ask for more things than you thank the Lord! You can thank him for your health, your family that loves you or the air that you breath, even the food that you're about to eat. There are many things that God does for us even when we don't know it. Don't just thank and ask for things when you pray, this is your time to spend with God.

Pray for the people that you see that are in need and or suffering from diseases, emotional trauma, inability, or mental illnesses. If you feel frustrated about something then talk to him about it, or talk about your day. When you have good days talk to him about it. When you have bad days vent to him about it. You have to pray for your enemies as well. Anyone who makes you angry, frustrated, or sad.

Soon there will be a time when this person feels what you've been feeling. You want to pray that God have mercy on them. What you think they might deserve, God can and will give them something more than sixty times worse. You may feel angry and want them to suffer. However God's word tells us to pray for our enemies. As difficult as it may seem you, don't want to wish anyone harm. Always allow the Lord to handle your enemies as he sees fit. He is the ultimate Judge and Jury.

Who is getting your prayer?

Have you heard of a god? Well there is a god and he goes by many names.

Examples:

The Father, God, All Mighty, Mungu, Jah, Heavenly Father, Lord

His son who has the power to do all things. His name is Jesus, and like God his son goes by many names as well.

Examples:

Jesus, Wonderful, Mighty God, Everlasting Father, Prince of Peace, Council, Holy Spirit, Messiah, Yesu, Lord, The Son of God

Jesus loves God's children, and only wants to please God. God makes sure you're family, friends, and you are safe. The Father could be in many forms he could be a plant or person, he only lets very few people see him.

How much does God love you?

God loves you, so much he brought his own son Jesus in the world and made him sacrifice himself for our sins. At the time Jesus was on the Earth people were doing evil deeds and there were very few good people in the world. At the rate mankind was going almost no one would be going to Heaven. God loves mankind and wanted them all to go to Heaven. Jesus was the only purely perfect creature that was a worthy sacrifice.

All Jesus wanted to do was please God, so Jesus went along with it. Jesus was killed on the cross, so we could have a chance to go to Heaven. That's how much God loves you. Think about having to sacrifice your own son or daughter for people's evil behaviors. Think about how painful that would be for you and your child.

He hated the thought of sacrificing Jesus, he tried numerous other ways to clean away people's sins. People were still sinning, so he brought Jesus to the World to spread the true message of God. After thirty five years of preaching with his disciples, Jesus died on the cross.

Praise singing

Another way to say thank you or say how much you love God and Jesus. You can praise sing. Praise singing is singing thanks or singing how much you love God. You can make up your own praise song too.

Glossary

Cross -A ✝ shaped object that were used to punish criminals in Rome.

Diseases - When you're not feeling well. (Having a cold, or fever)

Emotional trauma - When someone is dealing with something at home or in their own world that is causing them to be sad or unhappy.

Enemies - Someone who hates you and who is evil to you.

God - Your Heavenly Father.

Heaven - A beautiful wonderful place not for your body, but for your spirit.

Inability - Someone is missing a limb, like a arm, leg, or finger. Another example is being blind, deaf, or mute. (*Mute* means you can't speak)

Jesus - God's son.

Mental illnesses - When someone doesn't think right, or is mentally crazy.

Mercy - Going easy, or sparing.

Numerous - Many, a lot.

Prays Singing - When you're singing how much you love and appreciate God.

Preaching - Telling and persuading people to think or believe something.

Sins - Acts against God's will. (Evil behaviors)

About the Author

About Kasey

A fourteen year old girl who has a passion for God and Jesus. She wants to help others find and pray to them as well. She's made a book to help others find their ways and times to pray to God. She doesn't want to force the message of God and Jesus on anybody, but she wants to spread it to as many people as possible. She tries to be helpful to people of all ages.

She has written other narratives that are soon to be published. She likes to think of this book as the first few steps to help people find a relationship with God.

Printed in the United States
By Bookmasters